How To Draw
Baby Animals

How To Draw
Baby Animals

Author
Lisa Regan

Artist
Steve Roberts

Miles
Kelly
PUBLISHING

contents

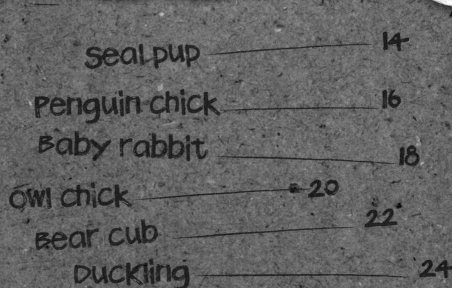

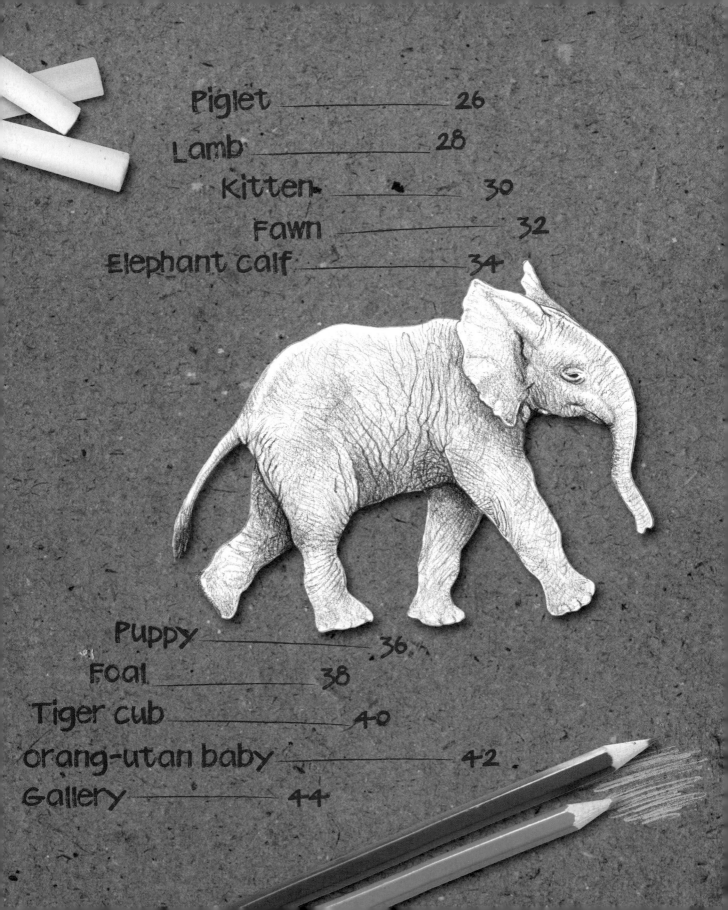

materials

DRAWING BABY ANIMALS ISN'T EASY, BUT FINDING THE MATERIALS TO GET YOU STARTED IS. YOUR BASIC ITEMS ARE PENCILS AND PAPER, BUT THERE ARE DIFFERENT KINDS TO CHOOSE FROM.

Colours

Many of your sketches will be in pencil as you practise drawing animal bodies. When you want to add colour, use crayons, pencils and watercolour paints or pencils. Coloured pencils are great for the soft colours and textures of baby animals.

Coloured pencils

The simplest way to add colour is with coloured pencils. Some can be blended with water to turn them into watercolours. You can also layer coloured pencils on top of each other to make new colours.

Pencils

Look for the letter marked on the side. B means a pencil makes soft, smudgy lines. H means it makes fine, harder lines. HB is in between.

Soft pencil

Hard pencil

Paper

Collect old paper and use it to practise on, making small sketches. As you get confident in your drawing skills, you can buy art paper for colour sketches and finished pictures. Try drawing on textured paper, such as handmade paper, for a softer effect.

corrugated paper adds extra depth to bumpy textures

Charcoal and chalk

Charcoal comes in black, brittle sticks, which can be smudged and blended easily to create shadowy, dramatic pictures. Chalk pastels are good for adding highlights, and are best used on coloured paper.

Felt-tip pens

Pens can be used to add a more cartoon-ish feel to your drawings. You can use them to define outlines and create dramatic patterns and markings.

Extras

You will also need a pencil sharpener, and a couple of erasers will be a great help. Choose a hard one for rubbing out lines, and a softer (putty) eraser for removing sections of colour or shading. It will help if you carry a sketch book at all times – a cheap, unlined notepad will do fine.

Buy handmade paper from gift or art shops

Textured papers make excellent backgrounds

Anatomy

To draw baby animals accurately, you'll have to unlearn what you think you know about animals and how they look. Work from real life whenever you can, drawing pets or animals at the zoo. It will also help to study photos or other artists' natural history drawings.

Use scrap paper or a sketchbook to do small, quick sketches of different animal body parts such as paws or heads, to refer to later.

Basic shapes

Start by looking at shapes and proportions — the first stages of the drawings in this book are designed to help you with this. Compare the body shapes of different baby animals and try to find similarities that will help you get started.

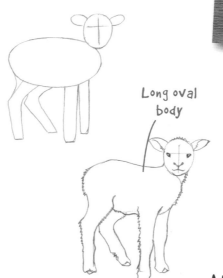

Long oval body

At first glance, a lamb and a foal look very different...

Rounded oval head

Four straight legs, each with one main joint

...but their basic anatomy has some similarities.

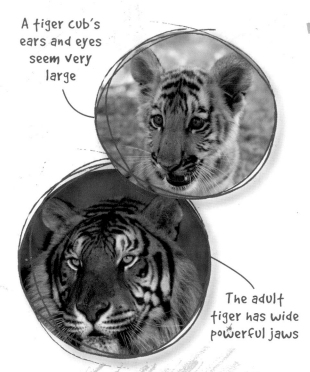

A tiger cub's ears and eyes seem very large

The adult tiger has wide powerful jaws

Making a scene

Many baby animals depend on their parents for everything. Very young orang-utans can do little more than cling to their mothers. Find some photos to copy and try drawing some mother and baby scenes.

The baby is clinging to its mother, so not all of its body is visible

Heads

Baby animals' heads sometimes seem to be almost too big for their bodies. Their muzzles are shorter than their parents' and their jaws are less pronounced.

Not only is the body bigger, it's also much more powerful

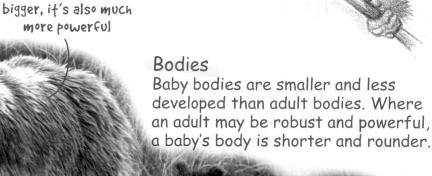

Bodies

Baby bodies are smaller and less developed than adult bodies. Where an adult may be robust and powerful, a baby's body is shorter and rounder.

The adult's huge, strong body makes its head look smaller by comparison

9

Action

Not only do baby animals have different proportions to their parents, but they also move in different ways. A young deer's legs are very thin and spindly, and it stands and walks in a very wobbly way, looking as though it isn't quite in control of its movements.

Back is bent

Head is lowered

Legs are spread wide to help stability

Leaping and falling

Many baby animals seem to have endless energy. They bound around, almost jumping instead of walking or running. Watch how a puppy or a kitten plays on the floor. Sometimes all four paws leave the ground at once!

Tail stretched out for balance

Stretching and grabbing

Drawing a few baby animals together in different positions, such as this nest of hungry chicks, gives the impression of lots of movement.

Mouths wide

Necks stretching

Perspective

Baby animals will leap around, changing direction all the time. This can help you to study perspective, which is our view of objects in relation to one another. Things look smaller when they are further away, and seem bigger up close.

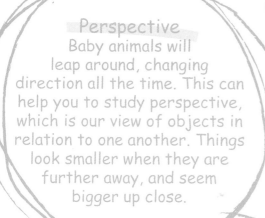

Side View

A side view shows true proportions. Although only one of the puppy's legs is completely visible, all four look the same length.

Front View

In a front view, the parts closest to you will appear much larger than those further away, so the puppy's front legs look longer than its back legs. The body also looks much shorter than it really is. This is known as 'foreshortening'.

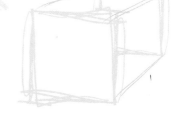

Taking a break

Baby animals may move fast, but they quickly tire themselves out, and they need a lot of sleep. This is definitely the easiest time to draw them — while they are still!

shading

DIFFERENT KINDS OF ANIMALS HAVE VERY DIFFERENT TEXTURES. PIGLETS ARE HAIRY, KITTENS ARE FURRY AND ELEPHANTS' THICK SKIN IS TOUGH AND WRINKLY. PENGUINS, DUCKS AND OWLS ALL GROW SMOOTH FEATHERS WITH AGE, BUT AS BABIES THEY'RE MORE FLUFFY, TOO.

Fine feathers
Very short pencil strokes show baby birds' downy texture.

Feathers and fur
You can show fur in your drawings, but don't worry about drawing every single tuft. Most of your drawings will have an outline that is at least partly smooth.

Colour shades
Scribble on scrap paper to make sure you have the correct shades of the colours you want. Gradually press harder with one colour to see what shades a single pencil can give.

Soft and smudgy
Pastels and charcoal can be smudged to look soft, like short hair.

12

Shadows and lights

An animal's colour is affected by light. Shadows make colours much darker. Experiment with browns, dark blues and black for your shadowed areas. When drawing from life, screw your eyes up and squint at the animal to see where the light and dark areas are. Leave white areas for shine.

Highlights

Shadows

Stippling

3-D shading

Use shading to add tone to your pictures and make them look more 3D. Colour lightly and press harder to get darker shades, or use stippling and hatching to add depth to your colours.

Cross-hatching

Hatching

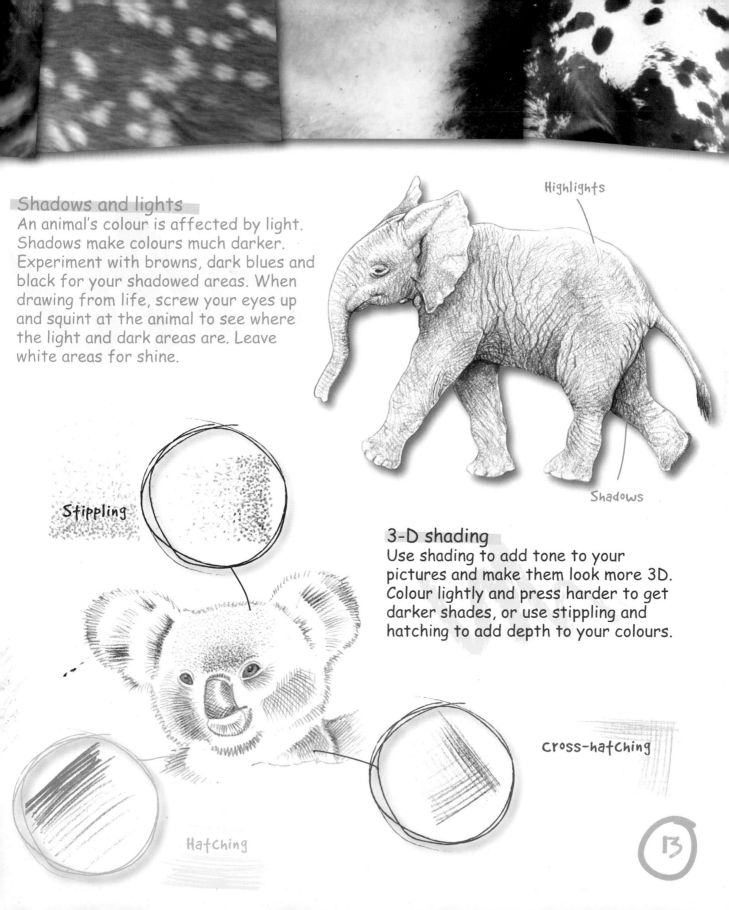

seal pup

1 Draw a large oval for the body and a smaller one for the head. Add a rounded shape at the back for the hind flipper and a narrow, curved shape for the front leg.

Mark in positioning line for the features

The pup is supporting itself on its front legs

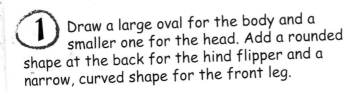

2 Shape the body and tail so they are one flowing shape.

Roughly sketch the large eyes and nose

Mark in the mouth

Add detail to the tail

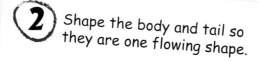
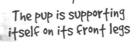

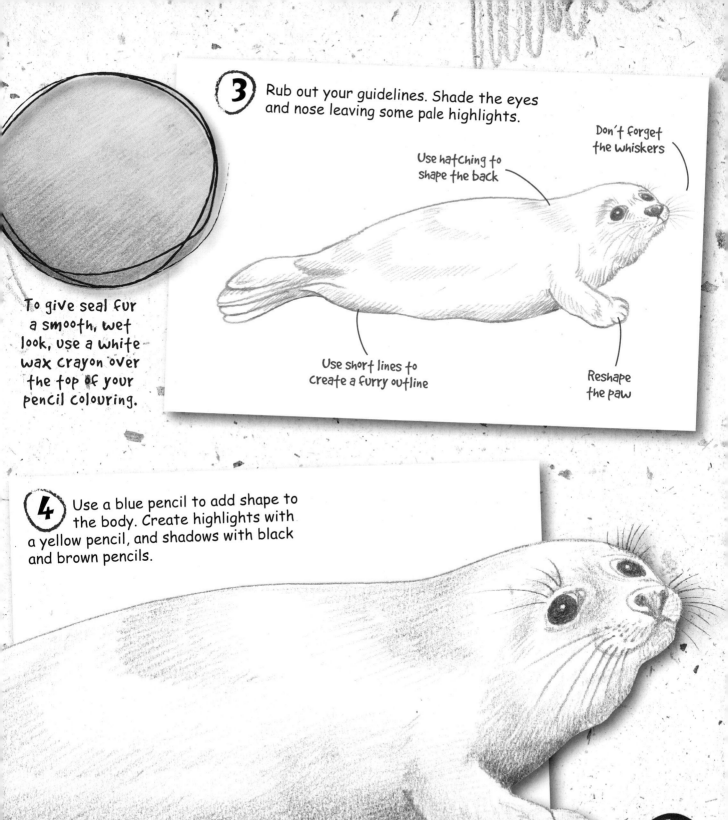

3 Rub out your guidelines. Shade the eyes and nose leaving some pale highlights.

Use hatching to shape the back

Don't forget the whiskers

Use short lines to create a furry outline

Reshape the paw

To give seal fur a smooth, wet look, use a white wax crayon over the top of your pencil colouring.

4 Use a blue pencil to add shape to the body. Create highlights with a yellow pencil, and shadows with black and brown pencils.

penguin chick

1 Draw a large egg shape for the body, with a small circle for the head.

Mark the positions of the eyes and beak

Shape the neck

Add rounded leg shapes

Adding detail using a white watercolour pencil over the top of regular coloured pencils gives more depth to shading.

2 Draw lines to show the markings on the head. Sketch in the eyes and beak. Add pointed shapes for the wings.

The wing shapes start at the end of the curve for the neck

Draw the claws

3 Shade the darker areas on the head and wings. Fill in the eyes and beak, leaving tiny highlights uncoloured.

Break up the outline with tiny, feathery pencil lines

Add detail to the claws

4 Build up colour gradually using lots of short pencil strokes in soft blue and grey. Add light yellow detail around the eyes. Shade the feet, leaving highlighted areas pale to make them look hard and shiny.

Use a regular pencil to add lines of detail

Baby rabbit

2 Reshape the body, paws and ears to give them a smoother, more defined shape.

Draw in the features

Add detail to the paws

1 Draw a large oval for the body and a smaller oval for the head.

The ears are triangles

Use a curved line to show the shape of the head

Add a line for the position of the eye

Add rounded shapes for the front legs and paws

The back legs and paws are more pointed

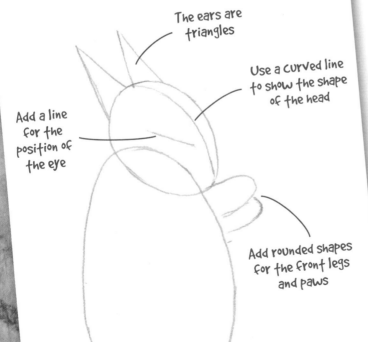

3 Shade the eye and nose. Add depth and shape by drawing rounded lines of short pencil strokes across the body.

The fur on the ears is very fine

Leave a highlight to make the eye look bright

Add long whiskers

4 Colour using light brown pencil. Draw thicker lines closer together to create darker tones for shaded areas. Use thinner lines further apart for lighter areas.

Leave the outline ragged to create a soft look

owl chick

1 Draw a circle for the head and a larger oval for the body. Roughly sketch in the shape of a branch along the bottom of the body.

Sketch a cross shape to help you position the eyes and beak

The claws are grasping the branch in two different ways

2 Add curved shapes for the wings, defining individual feathers towards the tips.

Sketch some detail around the eyes

Join the head and body with curved lines — the neck is short and wide

Much more of this wing is visible

To create the look of an owl's feathers by moonlight, use dark grey paper and add white pencil highlights.

20

3 Use a soft pencil to add lines of feathery detail on the head, body and wings.

Leave pale highlights so the beak and eyes shine

Add claws to this foot

Use scribbled lines on the branch to create texture

4 Colour in soft squiggly lines using red and brown pencils. Use black to highlight the darker sections of the feathers and claws.

The markings on the tips of the wings are now visible

21

Bear cub

1 Sketch the fat, rounded shapes of the body and head. Add four tapered leg shapes.

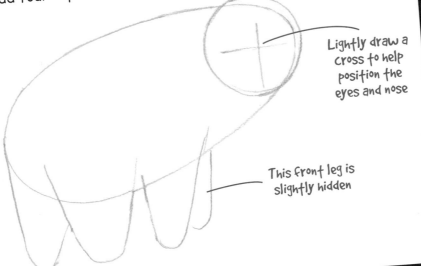

Lightly draw a cross to help position the eyes and nose

This front leg is slightly hidden

2 Shape the head to create a muzzle, and draw the ears, eyes, nose and mouth.

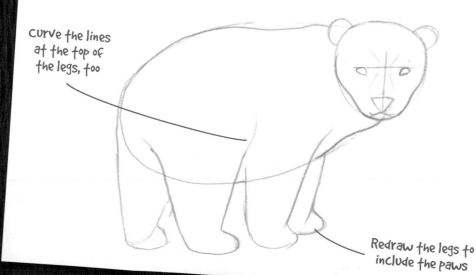

Curve the lines at the top of the legs, too

Redraw the legs to include the paws

3 Use firm lines to draw in the eyes, nose and mouth. Add short, soft lines of shadow, following the body shape, to give your drawing form and shading.

Use ragged lines to show the shape of the furry legs

Mixing pale blue pencil shades gives shape and shading to white fur.

4 This cub is a polar bear, so the colours are very soft. Use pale yellow and blue tones to add definition to the fur.

23

Duckling

1 Sketch a big oval body, a triangle for wings, and smaller ovals for the head and legs.

Leave space between the head and body for the neck

2 Draw in the neck and shape the head.

Start to shape the head

3 Shape the wings and legs and rub out your guidelines. Begin to add rounded lines to create detail on the body.

Add large eyes and a beak

Sketch triangles for the feet

Try using charcoal or pencil on rough paper, then smudge with your finger to create a soft, feathery effect.

4 Add texture to the body, wings, head and legs using soft, scribbled lines.

Give the beak more shape with shading

Add detail to the webbed feet

5 Add colour in rough lines to suggest the fine, soft feathers. Keep the outer lines rough and ragged.

Use orange, yellow and red for the beak, with black detail

Leave parts of the body white for highlights

25

Piglet

1 The pig's body shape is a long, sloping oval, with a smaller oval for the head. The legs are long triangles.

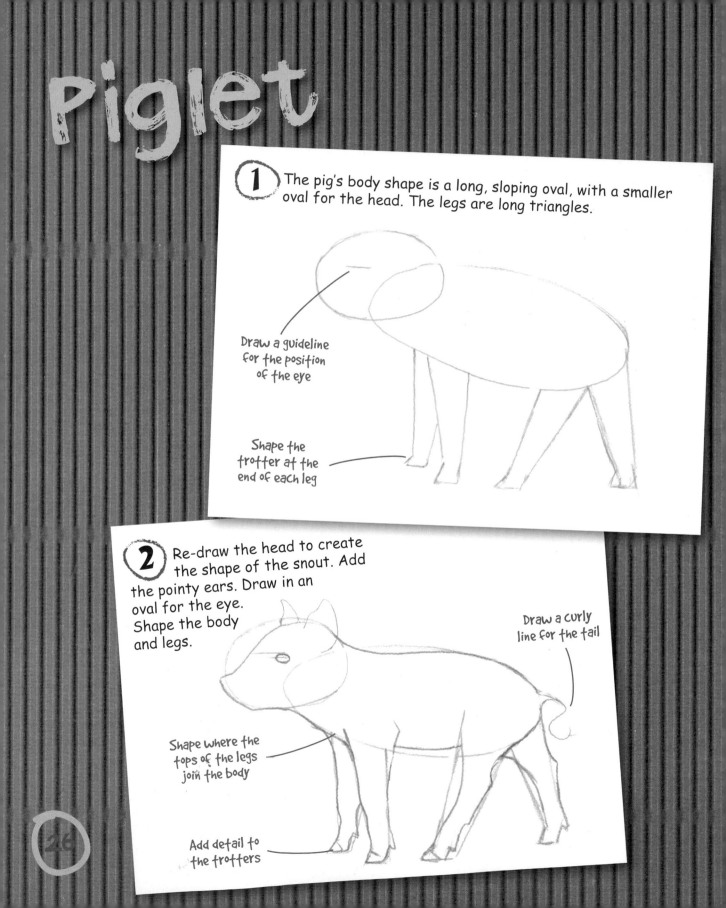

Draw a guideline for the position of the eye

Shape the trotter at the end of each leg

2 Re-draw the head to create the shape of the snout. Add the pointy ears. Draw in an oval for the eye. Shape the body and legs.

Draw a curly line for the tail

Shape where the tops of the legs join the body

Add detail to the trotters

3 Rub out any guidelines now. Define the ears, eyes and snout. Use hatched lines to create shadows on the tummy and legs.

Draw in a few wrinkle lines on the neck

Make the tail wider

Add a line for the mouth

4 Colour using pink and red – your pencil strokes should go in the same direction as the piglet's short, soft hair.

Use a pencil to define areas of shade

Lamb

1 A lamb has a horizontal oval body and a vertical oval head. The front legs are straight and the back legs are slightly bent.

Draw rounded shapes for the ears

Mark in a cross where the eyes, nose and mouth will be

2 Draw curved lines for the neck and give the ears more shape.

Start to add shape at the tops of the legs

3 Use short, ragged lines to reshape the body and legs. Rub out your guidelines.

The eyes are widely spaced

Draw lines for the nose and mouth

Add small hooves

4 Start to add lines of texture to the body. Shade the hooves.

Use rough lines to show the woolly texture

Create the stippled effect of fur with soft dots and squiggles in shades of brown.

5 With a brown pencil, colour in the legs and shade around the neck. Draw squiggly lines in pale blue and yellow pencils to add shape and texture over the body.

Leave some areas on the hooves white to add shine

kitten

1 Draw the oval body and head with the legs stretching forwards and backwards in action. Add the tail, which arches up over the back.

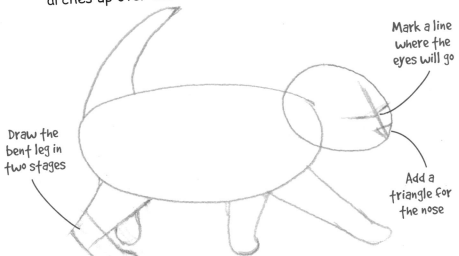

Mark a line where the eyes will go

Draw the bent leg in two stages

Add a triangle for the nose

2 Rework the body and head shapes to make them more sleek. Add more detail to the head and paws.

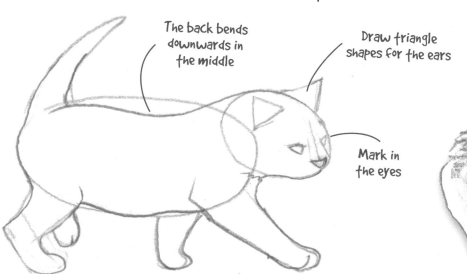

The back bends downwards in the middle

Draw triangle shapes for the ears

Mark in the eyes

3 Use a combination of long and short strokes to give shape and texture to the tail, legs and body.

A few darker lines indicate the markings on the fur

Short pencil strokes create a fluffy outline

Darken the eyes and nose

4 Add colour and markings with blue, brown and purple colouring pencils. Follow the direction of your pencil shading, and leave some areas white to create highlights.

Fawn

1 Use a combination of ovals to mark out the basic shape of the fawn lying down. Add the ears and a circle for the nose.

Mark a cross to show the position of the eyes

The neck is a curved line

The legs are bent underneath the body

2 Draw the curved lines of the back leg and rework the outline of the whole body, making it smoother. Start to add lines to give shape to the muzzle.

Redraw the ears

Add the outlines of the eyes

You can create the look of spotted fur by using dark brown as your base colour and leaving rough shapes white. Then use a lighter brown to blend the light and dark areas.

3 Use tiny, feathery lines to give more shape to the face. Rub out your guidelines now.

Add a line for the mouth

Leave a highlight on the shiny nose

Define the markings

4 Strong colour fills in the eyes and nose, with plenty of hatching on the face, ears and body to give them shape.

5 Mix red, brown and orange pencils to shade the fawn. Colour in the direction of the hair growth.

Elephant calf

2 Rework the head, adding the ear and trunk.

Shape the back

Draw in a thin tail

Give the legs more shape

1 Start your drawing with an egg-shaped body, triangular legs and a quarter-oval for the head.

The legs overlap at the top

This leg will be bent, so it's shorter

3 Rub out your guidelines and add the feet. Start to add shadow around the legs and neck.

Begin to add detail to the ear

Mark in the eye and mouth

The tail finishes in a brush shape

4 Start to hatch in wrinkles on the body. Use cross-hatching to make dark shadows on the neck and legs. Shape the toes.

The trunk has wrinkles, too

Add detail around the eye

To create the look of wrinkly skin, draw wavy lines, heavy in one direction and lighter across them.

5 Colour the skin with greys and browns, shading in lots of different directions. Add deeper wrinkles with a pencil.

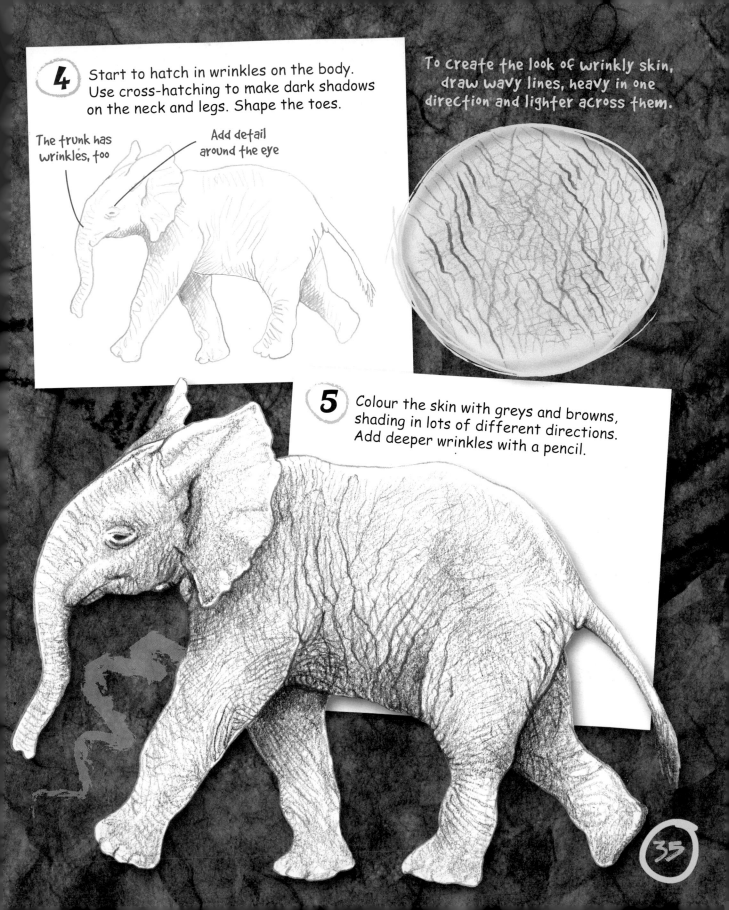

35

PUPPY

1 Draw an oval for the body. The oval should slope down because the puppy is facing towards us. Add another oval for the head and triangles for legs.

Add the tail

The body is wider near the head

Draw circles for paws

2 Draw in the ear shapes. Mark a cross on the face to position the eyes and nose.

Start to add shape at the tops of the legs

3 Rework the whole outline to make the body, tail and legs flow.

Define the eyes and mouth

Mark lightly on the head to get the muzzle shape right

Shape the paws

4 Add lots of hatching to show the shape of the back, stomach and legs.

Little lines make the fur look soft

Add whiskers

5 Colour the dog with a light brown pencil, with darker brown for shadows. Leave some areas white for highlights. Add detail to the head with a red pencil.

Foal

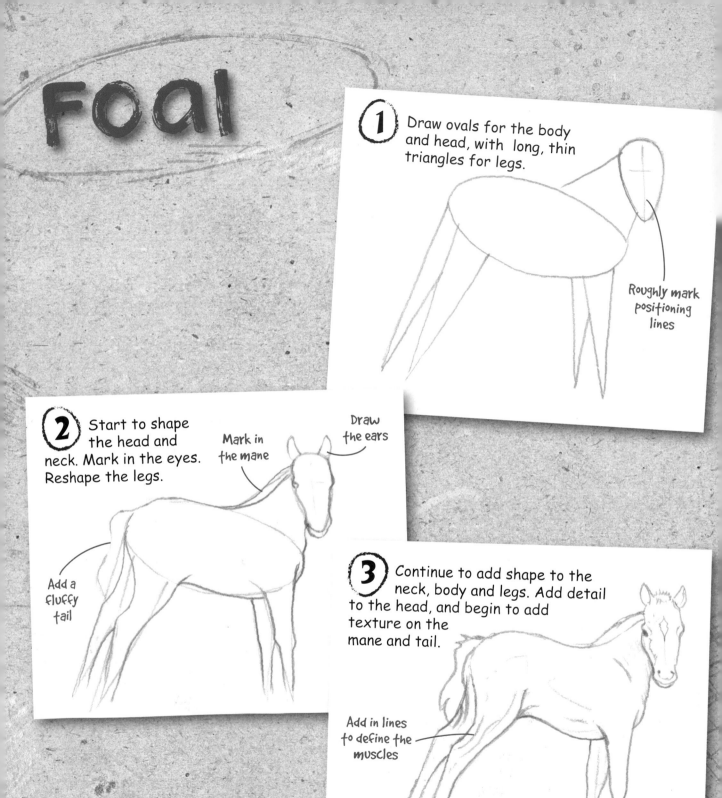

1 Draw ovals for the body and head, with long, thin triangles for legs.

Roughly mark positioning lines

2 Start to shape the head and neck. Mark in the eyes. Reshape the legs.

Mark in the mane

Draw the ears

Add a fluffy tail

3 Continue to add shape to the neck, body and legs. Add detail to the head, and begin to add texture on the mane and tail.

Add in lines to define the muscles

The hooves slant forwards

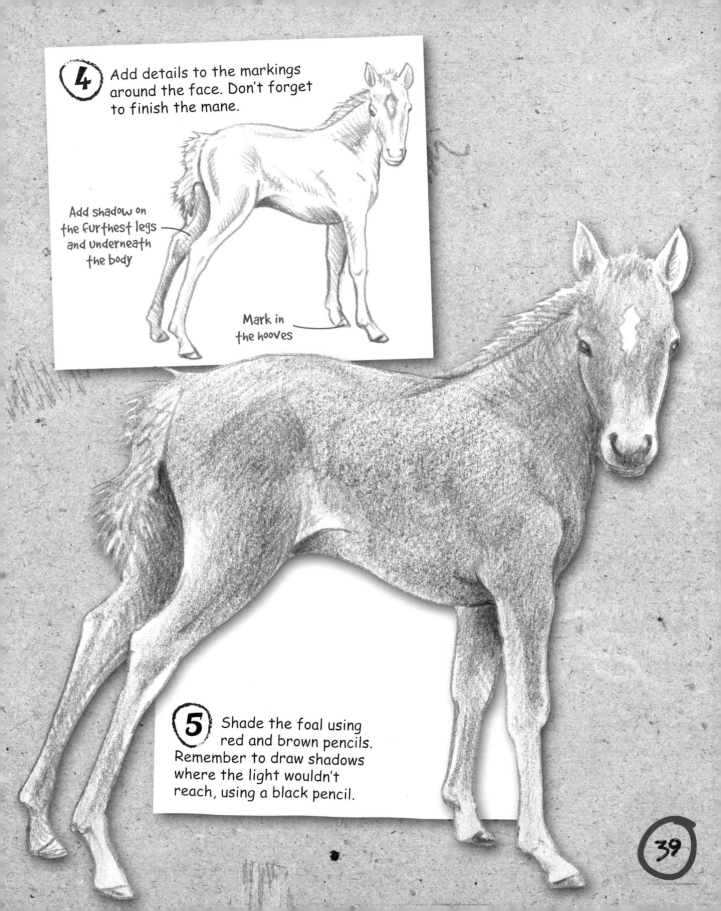

4 Add details to the markings around the face. Don't forget to finish the mane.

Add shadow on the furthest legs and underneath the body

Mark in the hooves

5 Shade the foal using red and brown pencils. Remember to draw shadows where the light wouldn't reach, using a black pencil.

Tiger cub

2 Mark in the eyes and a line for the mouth, and start to shape the muzzle and ears.

Draw a second front leg behind the first one

1 Draw an oval for the body – it's on a slant because the cub is sitting on a sloping surface. Draw the basic shapes of the head and ears.

Join the head to the body

A tiger's tail is much longer than a cat's

Draw two legs on the near side of the body

3 Use your guidelines to create a smooth, flowing line for the body, and then rub them out.

Continue to add detail to the head

4 Use bold lines for the stripes. Finish the detail on the face, adding whiskers and dark pupils in the eyes.

Draw ragged lines around the head to show the fur

Try drawing your tiger cub on red card, using yellow and black pencils to create the patterned fur.

5 Mix reds and oranges for the main body colour. Leave the fur white on the paws and the underside of the body. Shade the eyes a light brown, and add pink to the nose.

orang-utan baby

1 Start by drawing ovals for the body and head. The arms and legs are lines that stretch off in different directions.

Mark crosses where the features will go

2 Start to shape the flexible limbs and mark in the hands, feet and branches.

Sketch in the eyes and muzzle

The feet are much bigger than the hands

3 Use lots of long lines to show the furry outline of the body. Give more shape to the feet and hands.

continue the branch

Add dark eyes, dots for nostrils and shape the mouth

Add more shape to the legs

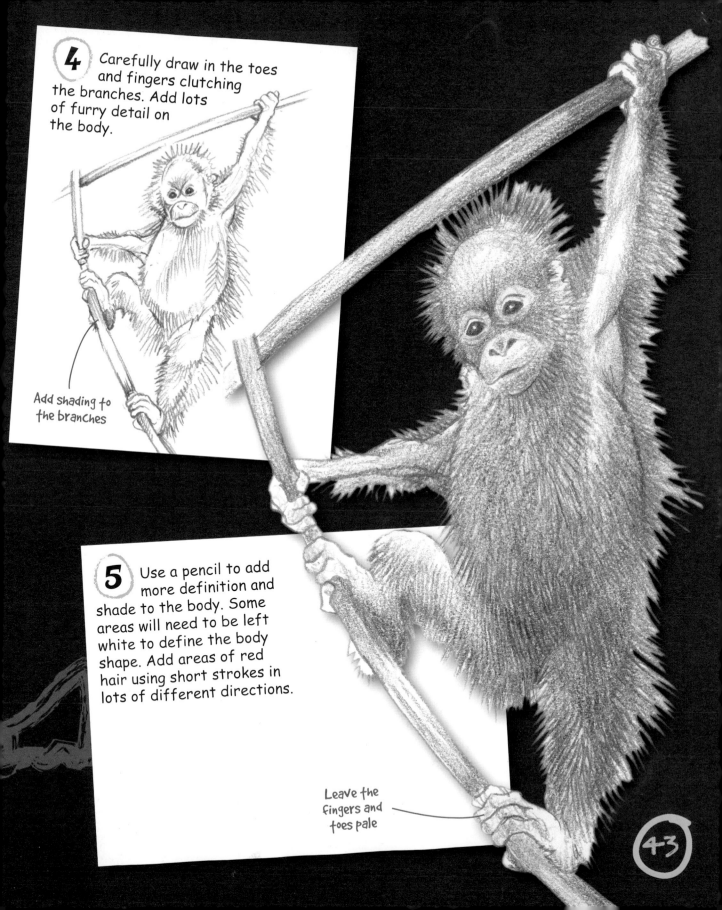

4 Carefully draw in the toes and fingers clutching the branches. Add lots of furry detail on the body.

Add shading to the branches

5 Use a pencil to add more definition and shade to the body. Some areas will need to be left white to define the body shape. Add areas of red hair using short strokes in lots of different directions.

Leave the fingers and toes pale

43

Gallery

Alligator hatchling

Fox cub

Chimpanzee baby
Study paws closely
to get them right.
This young chimp's
hands look almost
like human hands.

Chicks in a nest

Calf

Cheetah cub

Joey

45

Coot chick

Panda cub

Blue whale
mother and calf

Some baby animals are very
similar to their parents.

Puppy

46

Rhino mother
and calf

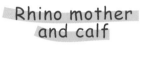

Young warthog

Have fun with poses. Show
your animals running in
different directions.

Emu chick

First published in 2008 by Miles Kelly Publishing Ltd
Bardfield Centre, Great Bardfield, Essex, CM7 4SL

2 4 6 8 10 9 7 5 3 1

EDITORIAL DIRECTOR Belinda Gallagher
ART DIRECTOR Jo Brewer
SENIOR EDITOR Rosie McGuire
EDITORIAL ASSISTANT Chlöe Schroeter
DESIGNER Simon Lee
PRODUCTION MANAGER Elizabeth Brunwin
REPROGRAPHICS Stephan Davis, Ian Paulyn

ISBN 978-1-84810-066-4

Printed in China

British Library Cataloguing-in-Publication Data
A catalogue record for this book is available from the British Library

ACKNOWLEDGEMENTS
The publishers would like to thank the following sources
for the use of their photographs:
Page 7 Feng Yu/Fotolia.com; 11 Joss/Fotolia.com

www.mileskelly.net
info@mileskelly.net